THE EMANCIPATION PROCLAMATION

ESSENTIAL LIBRARY OF

★ THE CIVIL ★
WAR

Essential Library

An Imprint of Abdo Publishing
abdopublishing.com

BY JUDY DODGE CUMMINGS

CONTENT CONSULTANT

MICHAEL DAVID COHEN
RESEARCH ASSISTANT PROFESSOR OF HISTORY
UNIVERSITY OF TENNESSEE, KNOXVILLE

abdopublishing.com

Published by Abdo Publishing, a division of ABDO, PO Box 398166, Minneapolis, Minnesota 55439. Copyright © 2017 by Abdo Consulting Group, Inc. International copyrights reserved in all countries. No part of this book may be reproduced in any form without written permission from the publisher. Essential Library™ is a trademark and logo of Abdo Publishing.

Printed in the United States of America, North Mankato, Minnesota

042016
092016

Cover Photo: Everett Historical/Shutterstock Images
Interior Photos: Everett Historical/Shutterstock Images, 1, 67; Heard & Moseley/Library of Congress, 4; Henry P. Moore/Library of Congress, 7; Schomburg Center for Research in Black Culture/Photographs and Prints Division/The New York Public Library, 9, 33; J. L. Magee/Library of Congress, 11; David Smart/Shutterstock Images, 12; Library of Congress, 14, 31, 49, 51, 56, 62, 85, 98 (left); North Wind Picture Archives, 17, 68; John Binns/Library of Congress, 19; US National Archives and Records Administration, 21; William L. Sheppard/Library of Congress, 23; Chas T. Webber/Library of Congress, 26; Universal Images Group North America LLC/Alamy, 29; Art and Picture Collection/The New York Public Library, 36, 39, 99 (top); Strobridge & Co. Lith/Library of Congress, 41; Public Domain, 43; AP Images, 45; George Stacy/Library of Congress, 46; Kurz & Allison/Library of Congress, 53, 89; Rainer Lesniewski/Shutterstock Images, 58; Alfred R. Waud/Library of Congress, 65; L. Prang & Co./Library of Congress, 71, 98 (right); Mathew Brady, 73; John Serz/Library of Congress, 76; L. Lipman/Library of Congress, 79; Thomas Kelly/Library of Congress, 86; Alexander Hay Ritchie/Library of Congress, 90; Harper's Weekly, 93, 99 (bottom); Carol M. Highsmith/Library of Congress, 96 (left), 96 (right)

Editor: Jenna Gleisner
Series Designers: Kelsey Oseid and Maggie Villaume

Cataloging-in-Publication Data

Names: Cummings, Judy Dodge, author.
Title: The Emancipation Proclamation / by Judy Dodge Cummings.
Description: Minneapolis, MN : Abdo Publishing, [2017] | Series: Essential library
    of the Civil War | Includes bibliographical references and index.
Identifiers: LCCN 2015960315 | ISBN 9781680782790 (lib. bdg.) |
    ISBN 9781680774689 (ebook)
Subjects: LCSH: United States. President (1861-1865 : Lincoln).--Emancipation
    Proclamation--Juvenile literature. | Lincoln, Abraham, 1809-1865--Views on
    slavery--Sources--Juvenile literature. | Slaves--Emancipation--United States--
    History--19th century--Sources--Juvenile literature.
Classification: DDC 973.7/14-dc23
LC record available at http://lccn.loc.gov/2015960315

CONTENTS

WATCH NIGHT

On December 31, 1862, people across the nation assembled in mansions and music halls, in schoolhouses and houses of worship, and in soldiers' tents and slave shanties. Church pews in cities across the North were packed with both African Americans and whites. This watch night began with prayers, followed by songs and speeches. Just before midnight, congregants knelt and bowed their heads. The church bells tolled 12 times, signaling the arrival of the New Year. Americans had anticipated this day for months—some with hope, others with dread.

The nation had been engulfed in the Civil War (1861–1865) since April 1861. Slavery was the root of the war. Northern states had abolished slavery decades earlier. However, the agricultural economy of the South depended on slave labor. Eleven southern

SLAVERY IN WORLD HISTORY

Slavery is as old as civilization. The holy books of Judaism, Christianity, and Islam all recognize slaves as a distinct social class. Even the ancient Greeks, who established the world's first democracy, practiced slavery. African slavery existed long before Europeans began exporting slaves to the Americas. In Africa, the slave class was composed of prisoners of war, people in debt, and criminals. Slavery in the United States was based on race, and American slaves were viewed as chattel, or property. American slaves had no more legal rights than a horse or a cow.

states ultimately seceded from the United States because they did not want the federal government to place any restrictions on their African-American slaves, whom the white Southerners considered their human property.

Almost two years into the conflict, the war had reached a bloody standstill. President Abraham Lincoln decided to use every weapon available to reunite the country, including the South's four million slaves.[1] On September 22, 1862, he forewarned the Confederate states: if they wanted to keep their slaves, they would need to lay down their weapons and rejoin the Union, because on January 1, 1863, he intended to sign the Emancipation Proclamation. This document would declare all slaves in rebelling states to be free people.

After making this shocking announcement, Lincoln was under intense pressure. In December, the Union army lost the Battle of Fredericksburg and suffered more than 13,000 casualties.[2] Conservatives urged Lincoln to abandon his emancipation plan, convinced it would enrage Southerners and prolong the war. Radicals criticized him for not immediately freeing all slaves everywhere

and demanded he expand the proclamation. As the end of the year drew near, Americans were uncertain about what the president would do.

TIME OF SORROW TRANSFORMED

Slave owners balanced their books at the end of the year. If they were in debt, they sold off some slaves on January 1. After Harriet Jacobs escaped from slavery, her 1861 memoir, *Incidents in the Life of a Slave Girl*, was published. In it, she describes the ache slave mothers must have felt for centuries. In Jacobs's recounting, on New Year's Eve, the mother "sits on her cold cabin floor, watching the children who may all be torn from her the next morning; and often does she wish that she and they might die before the day dawns."[3] Jacobs witnessed one woman lead all seven of her children to the auction block, where every one of them was sold away from her. For slave families, New Year's Eve was a time of grief, not of celebration.

However, December 31, 1862, was different. A night of dread was transformed into one of anticipation as it became known as Watch Night. A mostly African-American crowd congregated at Tremont Temple in Boston,

DEHUMANIZATION

In 1856, a journalist asked a white overseer how difficult it was to kill a slave. The overseer replied, "I wouldn't mind killing a [negro] more than I would a dog."[4] The institution of slavery dehumanized African Americans. This dehumanization of slaves allowed owners to justify the mistreatment and selling of human beings.

On December 31, 1862, 300 escaped slaves gathered in a camp on the outskirts of Washington, DC. These men and women sang and prayed into the dawn. One man, Thornton, sobbed the entire night. When asked why he was crying, Thornton said, "Tomorrow my child is to be sold [never] more."[6]

Massachusetts. As the New Year dawned, abolitionists and former slaves rallied the crowd with speeches. A human chain linked the nearest telegraph office to the speakers' platform at the church. When news was released that the proclamation had been signed, messengers planned to spread the word through the city to the anxious audience waiting in church. But the hours dragged by, and the telegraph wires remained silent. People began to despair. Perhaps President Lincoln had changed his mind.

Finally, in the middle of the afternoon, a man at the back of the temple cried out that the news had come. A local lawmaker read the official version of the Emancipation Proclamation aloud. It stated "all persons held as slaves"—within the rebellious states—"are, and henceforward shall be free."[5] People jumped to their feet, tossed their hats into the air, and shouted with joy.

Celebrations of what came to be known as the Year of Jubilee continued through the weekend. On Monday, January 5, a final celebration was held at Cooper Union, the New York hall where, three years earlier, Lincoln had given a speech that catapulted him to national attention. A band of African-American and white musicians played "The Star-Spangled Banner" to a packed auditorium.

The crowd gave three cheers for President Lincoln, three cheers for the flag, and three cheers for the abolitionists who had fought for decades to liberate the slaves.

However, not everyone rejoiced. The Emancipation Proclamation only freed slaves in the Confederate states. The Confederate army controlled this territory, so Lincoln had no real power to release these slaves. Slaves in the loyal states of Delaware, Kentucky, Maryland, and Missouri were not emancipated under the proclamation. Lincoln had also exempted other Confederate territory the Union army already occupied.

African-American abolitionist John Oliver wrote a letter about the slaves of

In time, the Emancipation Proclamation would apply to all slaves, regardless of the territory they lived in.

FREEDOM FOR ALL, BOTH BLACK AND WHITE!

The Emancipation Proclamation stands side-by-side with the Declaration of Independence as one of the cornerstones of US democracy.

Norfolk, Virginia. Thousands had gathered together on New Year's Day, believing their freedom was imminent. However, as the Emancipation Proclamation was read aloud, the slaves realized their region of Virginia was exempt from the rule. They remained in bondage. Oliver's letter described how the owners of these slaves told them "no one on earth has the power to free them."[7] Those slave owners were wrong.

The Emancipation Proclamation would eventually lead to the freedom of all slaves. However, abolition was not Lincoln's purpose in this declaration. Military victory was the purpose. When the Civil War began, President Lincoln's goal was to preserve the Union, not free the slaves. Yet, as the war progressed, Lincoln realized he could not do one without doing the other. To preserve the Union, he had to free the slaves. So the Emancipation Proclamation ultimately transformed the Civil War. A conflict focused on preservation evolved into one of liberation.

The Emancipation Proclamation was controversial in its day and is still oftentimes misunderstood. The act freed some slaves but left many in bondage. The writing style of the document is flat and bland, but Lincoln believed it to be "the central act of [his] administration, and the great event of the nineteenth century."[8]

MODERN WATCH NIGHT

More than 150 years have passed since President Lincoln issued the Emancipation Proclamation. However, the tradition of Watch Night continues among African-American Christians today. Every New Year's Eve, thousands gather for church services, a time for both reflection and thanksgiving. Five minutes before midnight, the congregation kneels and prays through the end of the old year and into the beginning of the new.

CHAPTER 2

SLAVERY AS AN INSTITUTION

In August 1619, the British ship *White Lion* docked at Jamestown, Virginia. Its cargo consisted of approximately 20 Africans.[1] The captain exchanged the prisoners for food and set sail, leaving behind the first captive African people in North America. These prisoners were quickly sold. This event marked the beginning of a system of racial slavery that lasted more than two centuries and impacted the lives of millions of African Americans.

TRANSFORMATION

Slavery was not based on race when British colonists first settled North America in the 1600s. Poor people—black, white, and native—worked side by side. These indentured servants were bound by a contract to work for a master for a specified number of years. While indentured, these laborers had few rights. However, after their contract expired, they received a parcel of land and were freed, regardless of their skin color.

The 1625 Virginia census listed a man called "Antonio the negro" as a servant. Antonio changed his name to Anthony Johnson and married an African-American woman who was also a servant. The couple completed their indenture contracts, raised four children, and bought a large estate, which they operated with the aid of at least one slave and white indentured servants.

Anthony Johnson's land purchase appears in the historical record of 1640 alongside a more ominous item. That same year, three servants ran away from the Virginia plantation where they were contracted to work. One servant was black and two were white. All three men were caught and sentenced to 30 lashes. The white men had four additional years of service added to their contracts as punishment. However, the court ordered John Punch, the lone black man, to "serve his said master . . . for the time of his natural life."[2] Punch was the first slave recorded in Virginia's history.

The link between slavery and race was gradual. British colonists believed it was wrong to enslave a Christian, the religion of most whites. Because American Indians and Africans were not Christians, enslaving them did not interfere with the colonists' moral views. However, as time progressed, Christianity spread

FREEDOM PETITIONS

Free and enslaved African Americans petitioned the Massachusetts legislature to end slavery in 1773 and 1774, and again in 1777. In 1773, petitioners appealed to the "Wisdom, Justice, and Goodness" of the lawmakers. In 1777, the writers said they shared "in Common with all other men a Natural and Unalienable Right to . . . freedom."[4] None of the petitions were granted. However, slavery was abolished in Massachusetts with a court decision in 1783.

among both American Indian and African populations, threatening the supply of free labor.

Lawmakers found a way around the dilemma of handling Christian slaves by simply changing the rules. Nonwhite slaves could change their religion, but they could not change their race. In 1682, Virginia passed a law creating a racial line dividing white servants and nonwhite slaves. This law declared that all servants imported into the colony, whether they were "negroes, moors [Muslim North Africans], mulattoes, or Indians," were considered slaves.[3] Slavery was linked to one permanent characteristic: skin color. To guarantee the slave supply line even further, all 13 British colonies created laws declaring that the child of an enslaved woman was also a slave. Perpetual bondage, just as skin color, became an inherited trait.

LIBERTY FOR SOME

On April 19, 1775, British soldiers fired on American militia, signaling the start of the American Revolutionary War (1775–1783). The rebellion had been brewing for a decade. Americans resented the British soldiers stationed in their towns and cities. The British government taxed American purchases of everyday items, and the colonists had no right to vote on these taxes. In the eyes of American patriots, the British were treating them like slaves. In 1776, leaders gathered in Philadelphia, Pennsylvania, and crafted the Declaration of Independence to explain why Americans wanted freedom from Britain. One phrase spotlights the heart of the American rebellion: "We hold these truths to be self-evident, that all men are created equal."[5]

Approximately 20 percent of the American population was enslaved at this

Although the Declaration of Independence states all men are created equal, the institution of slavery still stood in America.

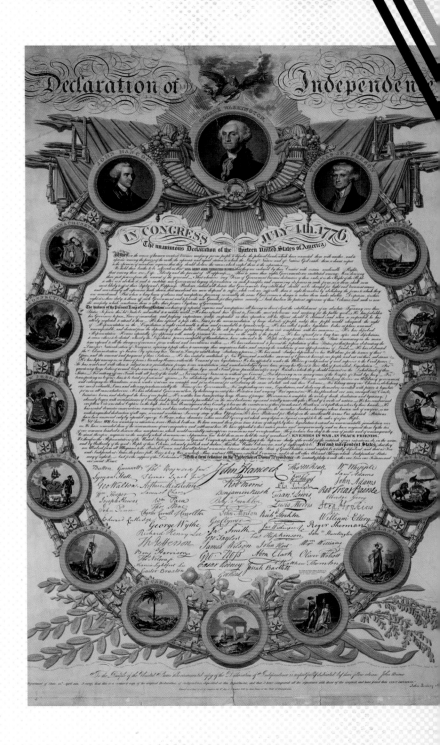

time, but the final draft of the Declaration of Independence contains only one reference to slavery: "He [King George III] has excited domestic Insurrections among us."[6] This statement referred to the actions of the British governor of Virginia, Lord Dunmore. In 1775, he offered slaves freedom if they fought for the British. Roughly 800 slaves joined Dunmore's regiment, and thousands more fled to British lines hoping to find freedom.[7]

Other slaves believed their chances for freedom were greater if the colonists won the war. Approximately 5,000 African-American men, free and slave, fought in the Continental army.[8] Their efforts helped lead America to victory in 1783. The United States of America became an independent country.

CHOOSING SIDES

Slaves sided with both the Americans and the British as they tried to gain freedom during the American Revolution. A slave named Titus fled from his New Jersey owner when he heard Lord Dunmore's proclamation. He became Colonel Tye and gained notoriety as a member of the Black Brigade, an elite group of African-American raiders who worked for the British Army. Prince Hall was a slave from Boston. Shortly after the American Revolution began, Hall's owner freed him so Hall could join the Continental army. Following the war, Hall became a leader in an organization for free blacks and spoke out against slavery.

However, as leaders worked to create a national government to unite the states, slavery was already dividing them.

When leaders gathered in Philadelphia in 1787 to draft a constitution, the divide between North and South was apparent. By this time, most Northern states had instituted plans to gradually abolish slavery. In the South, it was a different story. No Southern state, from Delaware to Georgia, had any plans to free its slaves.

At the Constitutional Convention, Southern delegates demanded protection for what they considered their human property. In most states, only white males who owned property could vote at this time, and because more whites lived in the North, these states would receive more representatives in Congress. Southern states balked at this, and the convention almost disintegrated. To save the infant nation, a compromise was reached. Even though slaves could not

The US Constitution also included a fugitive slave clause, which allowed owners to reclaim runaway slaves.

vote, each slave counted as three-fifths of a person for determining representation in Congress. This strategy kept the balance of power between free and slave states within the legislative branch. The Constitution, signed on September 17, 1787, guaranteed the international slave trade would continue for 20 more years. Leaders had made their first of many compromises concerning slavery.

EXPANSION

Slavery might have died a slow but natural death had it not been for Eli Whitney. In 1793, his invention of the cotton gin revolutionized the cotton-cleaning process. Suddenly, cotton became the king crop of the South and fueled the growing textile industry in the North. Within a decade, the US cotton crop went from an annual value of $150,000 to $8 million. With more cotton came more slaves. The 1790 federal census lists 697,897 slaves in the United States. By 1810, this number had skyrocketed to 1.2 million.[9] [10]

The cotton gin revolutionized cotton production and ensured the demand for slave

SLAVE BRUTALITY

Owners were legally allowed to whip, beat, mutilate, and even kill their slaves. In her memoir, Harriet Jacobs recounts the treatment a slave received after he tried to escape. The man was whipped 100 times, and then washed in saltwater before being placed inside a cotton gin with only enough room to flip from side to side. Each morning, bread and water were slipped inside the machine. After the fifth night, the screws of the cotton gin were removed. Inside, the slave was dead.[12]

As the number of slaves grew, the laws governing their lives hardened. Slaves could be bought, sold, leased, and inherited. A child born to a slave mother was a slave, no matter if that infant's father was the white slave owner. Between 1800 and 1860, more than one million slaves were sold from East Coast states to large plantations in the Deep South.[11]

In 1820, Congress passed the Missouri Compromise to maintain the balance of power between Free States and slave states. Missouri was admitted to the Union as a slave state; however, the law stated that from then on, any new territories below the 36° 30' north latitude line would be admitted as slave states. Any territories north of the line would be free.

In 1846, the United States went to war with Mexico, and two years later it won a vast tract of land in the southwest. A small but vocal abolitionist movement had developed by this time. These Americans began protesting the expansion of slavery into these territories even though they fell below the Missouri Compromise line. Senator Henry Clay fashioned a new compromise:

New Mexico and Utah could vote on whether they wanted to be Free States or slave states; the sale of slaves would be abolished in Washington, DC, although slavery would remain legal in that city; California would be admitted as a Free State; and a stricter Fugitive Slave Law would be passed. The nation was precariously balanced—half slave and half free. The scale was about to tip.

FUGITIVE SLAVE LAW

According to the 1850 Fugitive Slave Law, if a person was arrested on suspicion of being a fugitive, he did not receive a jury trial. Instead, a commissioner handled the case. These commissioners were paid five dollars for every alleged fugitive who was set free and ten dollars for each one turned over to the slave catcher making the claim. Therefore, the commissioners had a financial incentive to declare the person a runaway, even if he or she was free. All African Americans in the North felt threatened by this law. Throughout the following decade, 20,000 blacks fled to Canada.[13]

Southern cities, and others to isolated rural areas. Most runaways were single young men, such as Frederick Douglass. While working in a Baltimore shipyard, Douglass disguised himself as a sailor, borrowed a friend's certificate of freedom, and escaped to New York City.

Women were less likely than men to run, and enslaved mothers found escape particularly difficult. Mothers were reluctant to leave their children, and bringing children along on a flight endangered everyone in the group. However, slave families still attempted to run, sometimes with tragic consequences. In 1856, Margaret Garner, her husband, their four children, and her in-laws escaped to Ohio. When slave catchers apprehended the group, Garner slashed the throat of one of her children and tried to kill herself rather than return to slavery.

By the end of the 1700s, the Underground Railroad had evolved to aid runaways. The railroad was actually a vast network of people committed to helping fugitives. No single group ran this system. Brave people, both black and white, hid and transported fugitive slaves into Northern states or Canada. An estimated 100,000 Southern slaves escaped to freedom by means of the Underground Railroad between 1810 and 1850.[1]

FREDERICK DOUGLASS

1818–1895

Frederick Douglass spent his life fighting for freedom. Born a slave in Maryland in 1818, Douglass taught himself to read and write. He endured whippings and starvation from a brutal slave breaker before he escaped in 1838 and settled in Massachusetts. Douglass became a speaker for the Massachusetts Anti-Slavery Society and founded an abolitionist newspaper, the *North Star*.

Although Douglass frequently criticized President Lincoln's slow pace on emancipation, he recognized how important the Emancipation Proclamation was when Lincoln finally issued it. In February 1863, Douglass said, "We are all liberated by this proclamation. The white man is liberated, the black man is liberated."[2] Douglass actively recruited African-American men to enlist in the military, including his two sons. He also met with Lincoln personally to advocate for equal pay for black soldiers. Following the war, Douglass continued speaking for black equality, especially for the right to vote.

DARING ESCAPES

The historical record is rich with accounts of daring slave escapes. In 1848, married couple Ellen and William Craft freed themselves by hiding in plain sight. Ellen, a light-skinned woman, cut her hair short, dressed in men's clothing, and pretended to be a Southern cotton planter. Her husband, William, played the role of his master's obedient slave. On December 21, 1848, the couple traveled first class by train across Georgia and then boarded a steamboat to Charleston, South Carolina. En route, they even dined with the captain. The couple made it safely to Philadelphia and freedom.

Henry Brown mailed himself to freedom in 1849. A friendly storekeeper nailed Brown into a crate with a single airhole drilled in its side. Then the storekeeper mailed the crate from Richmond, Virginia, to the office of the Pennsylvania Anti-Slavery Society in Philadelphia. For approximately 27 hours, Brown lay in silence as the box was transported by hand, wagon, and train. When the crate reached its destination, workers at the society wrenched it open. They feared Brown had suffocated. Instead, a smiling, although sweaty, Brown sat up, held out his hand, and said, "How do you do, gentlemen?"[3]

INSURRECTION

On rare occasions, enslaved people rose up with force to demand their freedom. Nat Turner, a Virginian slave, experienced visions that he interpreted as God's directions to rise against his enemies. On a steamy summer night in 1831, Turner and six other slaves crept into their owner's house and killed the entire family. During the next few weeks, Turner's army grew to 40 slaves. Together, the army killed 57 whites. This rebellion provoked such hysteria throughout the South that white mobs murdered more than 200 innocent blacks.[4]

On October 16, 1859, white abolitionist John Brown led a raid on the armory at Harper's Ferry, Virginia. His goal was to seize weapons and launch a slave insurrection. The raid failed, and Brown and his men were captured. Southerners saw Brown's raid as proof that abolitionists wanted to destroy both slavery and slave owners.

ABOLITION

In the 1830s, a spirit of reform swept the nation, and a new radical movement was born: abolition. This crusade to end slavery began in September 1829 with the publication of a pamphlet referred to as David Walker's *Appeal*. Walker was the son of a free black woman and a slave father. He challenged white Americans to consider how slavery violated the Declaration of Independence. Walker urged slaves to fight for their freedom if necessary.

Turner was eventually caught and hanged, his corpse skinned. Another 55 slaves

Two years later, William Lloyd Garrison published the first issue of the *Liberator*, a newspaper destined to become a key voice of abolition. Garrison, a white man, wanted slaves to gain their freedom through peaceful means, but he used fiery language to shake up the system. In the first issue of the *Liberator*, Garrison wrote an editorial demanding that slavery end and free blacks get the right to vote. "I am in earnest," wrote Garrison. "I will not equivocate—I will not excuse—I will not retreat a single inch—AND I WILL BE HEARD."[5]

Garrison was part of the new generation of abolitionists who wanted slavery eliminated immediately throughout the nation. Women played a large role in this movement by circulating petitions and lecturing. Angelina Grimké Weld gave an impassioned speech in Pennsylvania in 1838 at the Anti-Slavery Convention of American Women. As an angry mob outside the hall pelted the windows with rocks, Weld told her audience, "Every man and every woman present may do something by showing that we fear not a mob . . . by opening our mouths for the dumb and pleading the cause of those who are ready to perish."[6]

While antislavery whites were motivated by empathy, many African-American abolitionists had an intimate understanding of the horrors of slavery because they had been slaves themselves. In 1843, former slave Henry Highland Garnet called on slaves to rise up against their owners and free themselves. Frederick Douglass did not support Garnet's call for violence, but he challenged whites on their definition of liberty. In 1852, Douglass gave a speech at a Fourth of July celebration. He questioned the crowd, asking why black people should honor such an occasion.

The abolitionists were a small minority in the North, but in the decade before the Civil War, they were joined by other voices. After the war with Mexico, US territory in the southwest ballooned. Opposition to the expansion of slavery in the West spread among Northern whites who desired land in these territories but feared they could not compete economically with slave labor. Debates over slavery occurred in parlors and taverns, in state houses and the White House. Soon, these debates would split the nation in two.

COLONIZATION

In 1817, a group of whites founded the American Colonization Society. Convinced Americans would accept emancipation more easily if free blacks were resettled outside of the United States, the group purchased land in West Africa. Most African Americans opposed colonization for reasons similar to Thomas Jennings's in 1828: "Our claims are on America; it is the land that gave us birth. . . . We know no other country, it is a land in which our fathers have suffered and toiled; they have watered it with their tears, and fanned it with sighs."[7] While 12,000 free blacks did settle the West African nation of Liberia, colonization was ultimately too impractical, too expensive, and too unpopular to work on a large scale.[8]

Confederate forces attacked the Union army at Fort Sumter beginning on April 12, 1861, signaling the start of the Civil War.

SLAVERY SPLITS THE NATION

On the night of April 12, 1861, slave owner Mary Chesnut could not sleep. Federal troops had been holed up in Fort Sumter, the federal military installation in Charleston Harbor, since South Carolina had seceded from the United States in December 1860. The Confederate government had warned Union major Robert Anderson that if he did not evacuate by 4:00 a.m. the next morning, they would bomb the fort. In the silence of the predawn, church bells tolled four times. Following the chimes, there was a brief silence, and Chesnut prayed nothing would follow. Seconds later, the boom of cannons shattered her prayers.

The bombardment lit the sky for 36 hours.[1] Then Union forces surrendered. This short, bloodless battle began the Civil War.

The next day, Chesnut studied the faces of her slaves. They showed no sign anything had changed. Chesnut wondered, "Are they stolidly stupid? Or wiser than we are; silent and strong, biding their time?"[2] American slaves had been biding their time for years. That was soon to change.

BLEEDING KANSAS

In 1853, Democratic senator Stephen Douglas proposed the Kansas-Nebraska Act and disrupted the fragile balance between slave states and Free States. Both Kansas and Nebraska territories lay above the Missouri Compromise line, and, therefore, should have been admitted to the Union as Free States. Instead, Douglas proposed the people of these territories should vote on the issue themselves. The bill became law on May 30, 1854, and Kansas exploded into a miniature civil war.

Proslavery fighters spilled over the Missouri boundary into Kansas. Simultaneously, more than 1,000 antislavery emigrants moved from Massachusetts to Kansas.[3] Both groups intended to stack votes in their favor, using violence to persuade people if necessary. People kidnapped, tortured, and murdered their opponents. The bloodshed in Kansas was a preview of what was to come on a much larger scale.

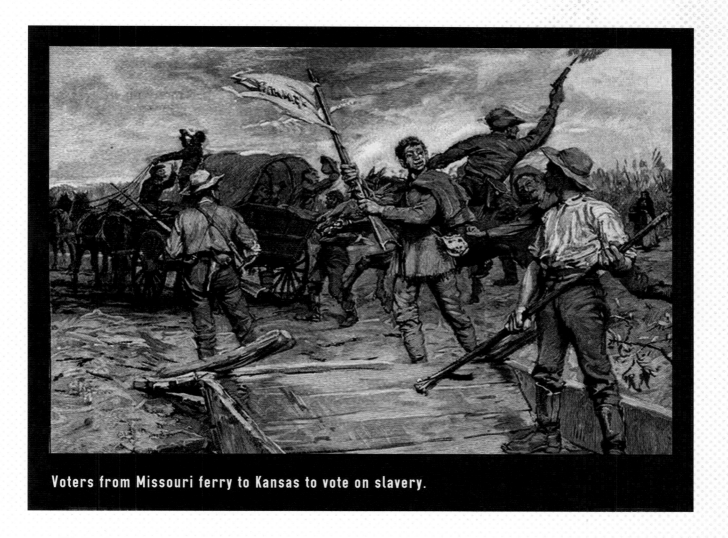

Voters from Missouri ferry to Kansas to vote on slavery.

ELECTION AND SECESSION

In October 1859, a lawyer from Illinois took the stage in front of 1,500 people in the Great Hall at the Cooper Union in New York. Abraham Lincoln was a Republican. This new party had been formed to prevent the spread of slavery

DRED SCOTT

In 1857, the Supreme Court issued a landmark decision that struck a blow against freedom. A Missouri slave, Dred Scott, sued for freedom because his owner had taken Scott to live in Illinois and Wisconsin, both Free States. The Supreme Court declared that as a negro, Scott was not a citizen of the United States and had no right to sue in court. The court also ruled slaves were private property and their owners could take them anywhere, even Free States.

into the western territories gained from the war with Mexico. People were not quite sure what to make of Lincoln at first. One eyewitness said "When Lincoln rose to speak, I was greatly disappointed. He was tall, tall,—oh, how tall! and so angular and awkward that I had . . . a feeling of pity for so ungainly a man."[4]

But when Lincoln spoke, he transfixed the audience. With the use of reason and evidence, Lincoln insisted the Republican Party's views on slavery were guided by the Constitution. He verbally dissected the Constitution to prove the Founding Fathers wanted Congress to control slavery rather than let it expand indefinitely.

Lincoln opposed slavery, but he was not an abolitionist. He believed slavery denied a man his most basic liberty—the right of receiving payment for work. However, Lincoln recognized the Constitution gave states the power to regulate their own internal institutions. Therefore, the federal government had no legal right to interfere with slavery where it already existed. As Lincoln campaigned for president in 1860, he insisted he would not obstruct slavery in the Southern

ABRAHAM LINCOLN

1809–1865

In 1809, Abraham Lincoln was born to a poor farming family in Kentucky. Lincoln attended less than a year of formal school during his life, but he hungrily read whenever he had the chance. When he was in his early twenties, he moved to Illinois, taught himself law, and entered local and state politics.

Lincoln opposed slavery all his life. As a young man, he visited New Orleans, Louisiana, and was traumatized by the sight of slaves on a chain. While serving in the Illinois state legislature, Lincoln signed a resolution condemning slavery. As a member of the House of Representatives, he condemned the Mexican War because he feared the expansion of slavery into new territory gained by the war. In 1864, Lincoln said, "I am naturally anti-slavery. If slavery is not wrong, nothing is wrong. I cannot remember when I did not so think, and feel."[5]

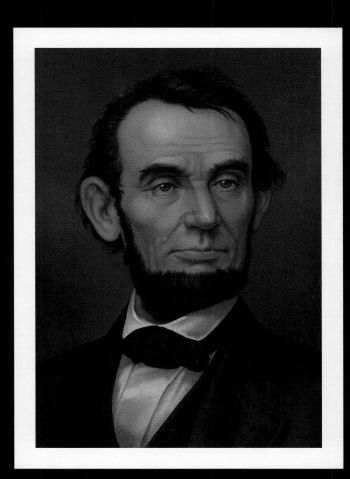

states. But he did maintain that the nation could not remain permanently divided as a half-free, half-slave country.

Southern slave owners feared Lincoln was right, and they were determined to resist any attempts by the federal government to restrict the growth of slavery. As the election of 1860 drew near, Southern planters fanned the flames of public hysteria. Rumors of slave insurrections and abolitionist plots ran in the headlines of Southern papers. Although he was not even on ten of the 15 slave state ballots and was defeated in the five where he was listed, Lincoln was elected president on November 6. Six weeks later, on December 20, South Carolina seceded from the United States. Other slave states soon followed.

CONGRESSIONAL BATTLES

Leading up to the Civil War, violence over slavery reached even the halls of Congress. In 1856, Massachusetts senator Charles Sumner gave a fiery speech condemning proslavery senators, including Andrew Butler from South Carolina. Butler's nephew, Congressman Preston Brooks, cornered Sumner at his desk in the Senate chamber and beat him unconscious with a gold-handled cane.

REVOLUTION OR REBELLION

In February 1861, the leaders of the seceded states met in Montgomery, Alabama, to form the government of the newly formed Confederate States of America. Former Mississippi senator Jefferson Davis was elected president.

The Confederate Constitution was modeled after the US Constitution, except for one main difference: slavery was protected.

The inaugural speeches of the two American presidents revealed a striking contrast. On February 18, 1861, Davis used the Declaration of Independence to justify secession. If the government harms the people it was created to protect, he argued, then the people have the right to abolish that government. Davis cast Southern secession as a revolution. According to this logic, if war broke out, he would be the president of a foreign power.

Confederate president Davis delivers his inauguration speech in Montgomery, Alabama, on February 18, 1861.

Lincoln did not grant Davis that status. He believed secession was illegal, and he classified the Confederate states as rebels, not a foreign power. Lincoln argued the US Constitution made the national government supreme over the states. Revolutions were reserved for people whose liberties were being trampled. Lincoln insisted he had not trampled on any Southerner's liberty.

Lincoln extended a friendly hand to the South in his inaugural speech. He again pledged not to interfere with slavery where it already existed, and he vowed not to strike the first blow. The Confederates did not trust Lincoln. They struck first at Fort Sumter on April 12, 1861. The Civil War had begun.

President Lincoln immediately committed himself to fighting a war to preserve the Union. It was not to be a conflict about slavery. However, slavery inserted itself into the fight from the very beginning and could not be ignored. Lincoln may have wanted to fight a war of reunification, but the Civil War would soon become a war of emancipation.

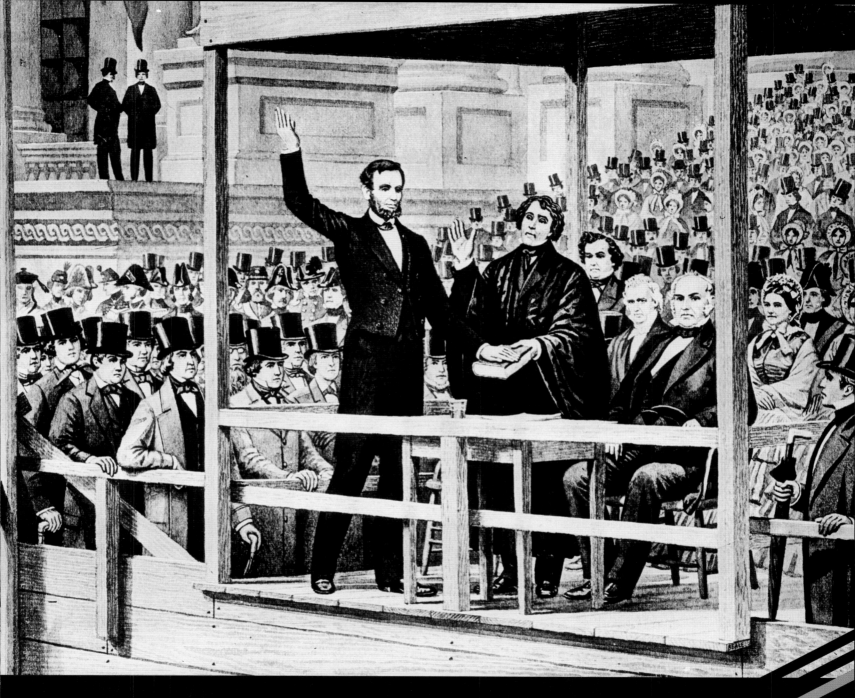

President Lincoln takes the oath of office at his first inauguration on March 4, 1861, at the US Capitol.

Fort Monroe came to be called the Freedom Fortress as slaves found refuge within its walls.

TO SAVE THE UNION

Frank Baker, Shepard Mallory, and James Townsend were slaves owned by Charles Mallory, a colonel in the Confederate army. In May 1861, Charles Mallory ordered the trio to dig artillery embankments near the mouth of the Chesapeake Bay. Just across the James River, they could see the Union-held Fort Monroe. On the night of May 23, the men silently slid a boat into the river and rowed for freedom. The Civil War was barely a month old. The Fugitive Slave Law required all escaped slaves to be returned to their owners. As Baker, Mallory, and Townsend entered the gates of the Union fort, they did not know what fate awaited them— freedom or a return to enslavement.

NOT A WAR FOR EMANCIPATION

After Confederates attacked Fort Sumter, Lincoln called for 75,000 volunteer militia to suppress the Confederate rebellion. Despite this aggressive move, Lincoln publically promised the federal militia would "avoid any devastation, any destruction of, or interference with, property."[1] Lincoln did not intend to interfere with Southern slavery.

While the president believed the Constitution protected slavery, he also had practical reasons for his position. After Lincoln's call for troops, four more slave states seceded. By the summer of 1861, there were 11 states in the Confederacy. Four slave states formed the border between North and South: Maryland, Missouri, Kentucky, and Delaware. They remained loyal to the Union, but this loyalty was fragile. Lincoln feared one wrong move could propel these states into the Confederacy. Maryland partly shielded Washington, DC, from Confederate territory; Kentucky offered invasion routes into the Confederacy; and Missouri was strategically located along the Mississippi River. Lincoln could not afford to lose these states.

Foreign policy also concerned Lincoln. The United Kingdom imported 80 percent of its cotton from the Confederacy.[2] In the first months of the war, Lincoln had ordered the Union navy to blockade all Southern ports. The South could no longer export or import goods to or from Europe. Southern leaders

Blockade runners, such as the *Chicora*, seldom evaded the Union forces when trying to transport Southern goods.

had been lobbying hard for the United Kingdom to aid them in breaking this blockade. Because the United Kingdom had huge stockpiles of cotton, it was not in a hurry to enter the war and declared neutrality. That status could change. Lincoln hoped that by treating the conflict as a domestic rebellion rather than a war, the United Kingdom would be reluctant to intervene. However, this strategy meant Lincoln could not treat the Confederacy as an enemy nation. Southerners were still citizens of the United States and retained their full constitutional rights, including the right to own slaves.

The special session of the Thirty-Seventh Congress, which convened on July 4, 1861, agreed with Lincoln about the purpose of the war. One of its first tasks was to issue a joint declaration: the United States was at war to maintain the supremacy of the Constitution and preserve the Union. The resolution specifically stated the war was not being conducted to interfere with state institutions—namely, slavery.

CONTRABANDS

Baker, Mallory, and Townsend—the three slaves who sought refuge in Fort Monroe—complicated the government's clear-cut war goals. According to the Fugitive Slave Law, the men should have been returned to their owner. But when Major General Benjamin Butler interrogated the slaves, they gave him useful information about the Confederate fortifications the slaves had been building. When Confederate major John Baytop Cary arrived at the front gate to retrieve the fugitives, Butler refused. Butler was a licensed lawyer. According to military law, a commander could seize enemy property being used for military purposes. The slaves had been building Confederate fortifications, so Butler considered them fair game for confiscation.

A few days later, eight more slaves arrived at the fort. These were followed by another 47, including children, women, and elderly.[3] News of refuge spread

In what came to be known as the Fort Monroe Doctrine, more and more slaves escaped the Fugitive Slave Law within Fort Monroe's walls.

among slaves across the country. By June, 500 fugitives had sought sanctuary inside its walls.[4]

Lincoln let Butler's action stand. By declaring fugitive slaves contraband of war, the general had found a way around the Fugitive Slave Law. However, Lincoln cautioned Butler to remember, "the business you are sent upon . . . is war, not emancipation."[5] Newspapers picked up on the word *contraband*, and the

FUGITIVE SLAVES RETURNED

Not all Union generals gave runaways refuge. Jack Scroggins was the slave of Maryland planter Samuel Cox. Scroggins told the Union troops camped near Cox's plantation that his owner had a hidden supply of arms and ammunition. When the Union army moved on, Scroggins went with them. Cox pursued the troops and demanded his slave back. At first, federal soldiers refused, but their officers told them they had to turn over the slave or they would be shot. The soldiers complied. Cox took Scroggins, dragged him behind a horse for 11 miles (18 km), and then beat him to death.

label stuck. No one, including the fugitives, knew if contrabands were slaves or free people. They were in a state of legal limbo.

However, the destruction of slavery had begun, led by the slaves themselves. Fugitives from Virginia in the north, to the Mississippi River in the west, to Florida in the south ran to Union lines. Some military commanders sent these escapees back to their owners. Slaves who did not run worked to undermine the institution from within. As Southern men went off to war, white women left in charge of plantations encountered slaves who refused to work or who did so slowly and reluctantly. Slaves were transforming the war into a conflict of personal liberation. Political leaders would slowly follow their lead.

MILITARY DEFEAT SPURS CONGRESSIONAL ACTION

No one was killed at the Battle of Fort Sumter, and Americans convinced themselves the war would be short and relatively bloodless. The First Battle of Bull Run on July 21, 1861, proved otherwise. The little creek called Bull

The First Battle of Bull Run proved to be a devastating blow for Union troops.

Run flows near the Virginian town of Manassas, which is approximately 25 miles (40 km) from Washington, DC. Union troops were confident as they marched toward the town's railroad link on July 16, 1861. They stopped to pick blackberries on the warm summer day, oblivious to the danger that lay ahead. Most of the soldiers were volunteers who had never seen combat.

By the time Union troops reached their destination, days had passed and 34,000 Confederate soldiers awaited them on the other side of the creek.[6]

FORCED TO FIGHT

John Parker and three other African-American slaves were in the ranks of Confederate soldiers at Bull Run. Parker had not wanted to carry a weapon for the South, but his owner had ordered him to fight. After the war, he said, "We wish[ed] to our hearts that the Yankees would whip [the Confederates] and we would have run over to their side but our officers would have shot us if we had made the attempt."[7]

At first, the battle progressed in the North's favor, but then Confederate general Stonewall Jackson's brigade launched a countercharge. The battle continued throughout the afternoon. Finally, clever flanking maneuvers by the Confederate commanders forced the inexperienced Union soldiers into a humiliating retreat back to Washington.

Northern politicians looked for someone to blame for the Union defeat. Rumors floated that thousands of slaves had been working for the Confederacy. John Parker, a slave forced to fight, was part of a small handful of slaves who had actually wielded a weapon, but scores of others performed manual labor that freed rebel soldiers to train and fight. Congress decided to remove slaves as a weapon in the arsenal of the Confederate army.

After a bitter debate, Congress approved the First Confiscation Act on August 6, 1861. This law authorized the government to confiscate slaves used to aid the Confederate war effort. Democrats opposed the bill because they feared such confiscation would eventually lead to an influx of free blacks into the North, who would take jobs from whites. Representatives from the Border States also disapproved of the bill. They worried confiscation was the first step toward emancipation. However, Radical Republicans outnumbered both these groups. These Republicans were members of Lincoln's own party who persistently demanded immediate and full emancipation for slaves as well as civil rights for free African Americans. One noted Radical Republican was Thaddeus Stevens. With the support of Stevens and the Radical Republicans, the First Confiscation Act passed. Worried about the reaction of the Border States, Lincoln reluctantly signed it.

FREEDOM REVOKED

Some military leaders moved quicker than their commander in chief on the issue of emancipation. General John Frémont commanded Union forces in Missouri. On August 30, 1861, he declared all slaves owned by Missouri Confederates free. Because Frémont did not just target slaves used by the rebel army, and because he emancipated slaves instead of calling them contraband, Lincoln declared Frémont's actions illegal. At the time, the Kentucky legislature was debating whether to secede. Lincoln feared Frémont's declaration would "alarm our Southern Union friends, and turn them against us—perhaps ruin our rather fair prospect for [Kentucky]."[8] Indeed, when they heard Frémont had freed Missouri's slaves, a company of Kentucky volunteers threw down their weapons and quit the

THADDEUS STEVENS

1792–1868

One of the most radical of the Radical Republicans, Thaddeus Stevens devoted his career to abolishing slavery. During the Civil War, Stevens chaired the House Ways and Means Committee, a powerful position that controlled the government's spending. His leadership helped pass the First Confiscation Act in 1861 and a law authorizing 150,000 black troops in 1862.[9] Stevens unceasingly pressured the president to issue an emancipation proclamation. Stevens helped draft the Thirteenth Amendment, and on January 13, 1865, he gave the closing remarks that ended the debate on this amendment. Stevens said if opponents supported the constitutional change, the war would end. But if they opposed it, the bloodshed would continue and "may the ghosts of the slaughtered victims sit heavily upon the souls of those who cause it."[10] The amendment passed, and slavery was abolished. Stevens remained in Congress until his death in 1868.

army. Lincoln ordered Frémont to rescind his emancipation order in September 1861.

GRADUAL EMANCIPATION

By the end of 1861, Lincoln faced increasing pressure from his own party to end slavery. When he addressed Congress on December 3, 1861, the president reminded lawmakers the purpose of the war was to restore the Union. His job as commander in chief was to manage the war. Slavery was Congress's burden to solve.

LINCOLN'S HINT

In May 1862, General David Hunter declared slaves in the sections of South Carolina, Georgia, and Florida that he controlled were forever free. Ten days later, Lincoln revoked this decision. In a public statement, he said that, as commander in chief, he reserved the right to free slaves if it became a military necessity. While the president faced a flood of criticism for not supporting Hunter's order, others found hope in his words. Lincoln had hinted emancipation might be militarily necessary someday.

Lincoln admitted the war had dealt slavery "a mortal wound," and he knew this erosion worried the Border States. Therefore, Lincoln proposed these states turn their slaves over to the government in lieu of paying their state taxes. Lincoln would emancipate these slaves and send them to Liberia or Haiti. He tried to convince his audience: "The emigration of colored men," said Lincoln, "leaves additional room for white men."[11] The Border States were not convinced, and abolitionists denounced the president's slow pace on emancipation. As 1861 drew to a close, the war continued, one bloody day after another.

BRITISH NORTH AMERICA

New Hampshire

Vermont

Oregon

Minnesota

Michigan

Washington
Territory

Dakota Territory

Wisconsin

New York

Nevada
Territory

Nebraska Territory

Iowa

Pennsylvania

Utah
Territory

Ohio

Colorado
Territory

Illinois

Kansas

Indiana

West
Virginia

California

Missouri

Kentucky

Virginia

New Mexico
Territory

Indian
Territory

Tennessee

North Carolina

Arkansas

South
Carolina

Georgia

Texas

Alabama

Mississippi

Pacific

Ocean

Louisiana

Florida

Union states without slavery

Union states and regions with slavery

MEXICO

Gulf of Mexico

Confederate states

Territories

N
W   E
S

CUBA

Maine

Massachusetts
Rhode
Island
Connecticut

New Jersey

Delaware
Maryland

Atlantic

Ocean

THE
BAHAMAS

A MILITARY MEASURE

In the winter of 1862, the Union received news that buoyed their spirits. General Ulysses S. Grant had surrounded Fort Donelson, a key Confederate installation on the Kentucky-Tennessee border. On February 16, the Confederate commander requested a meeting with Grant to discuss surrender terms. Grant's reply was simple: The only term he would accept was surrender. The rebels inside gave up. The Union suddenly had both a hero and a firm grip on Kentucky. President Lincoln seized this opportunity to renew his efforts to entice the Border States to free their slaves. His hope was that if these states initiated emancipation plans, the Confederacy would realize how isolated it was and end the rebellion.

COMPENSATED EMANCIPATION

In March 1862, Lincoln asked Congress to offer a pot of money to the Border States to use as they pleased as long as they initiated emancipation plans. He preferred a slow approach to freeing the slaves.

The reaction to Lincoln's proposal from antislavery advocates was mixed. Abolitionist Frederick Douglass saw Lincoln trying to walk a tightrope between Americans who opposed any kind of emancipation and those who wanted slaves freed immediately. Other abolitionists were disappointed with the limited scope of Lincoln's proposal.

On March 10, Lincoln met with a delegation from the Border States to persuade them to consider his proposal. He said that as long as the Union armies were in the field, slaves would flee to these armies, so the Border States were already losing their slaves. Lincoln said that while he was sensitive to the demands from Union slaveholders for the return of their runaways, such demands irritated

DIVIDED CONGRESS

The congressional debate over a bill to compensate the Border States for gradually emancipating slaves revealed deep divisions in the North. Some legislators opposed the bill because it did not address what to do with slaves after they were freed; others opposed it because the emancipation process would be too slow. Representative Thaddeus Stevens called Lincoln's proposal "the most diluted, milk and water gruel proposition that was ever given to the American nation."[1]

opponents of slavery, annoyed him, and were "embarrassing to the progress of the war."[2]

After intense debate, Congress eventually passed Lincoln's compensation bill, but no Border State initiated an emancipation plan. When the president saw the strong controversy this modest proposal generated, he reconsidered his strategy. Instead of targeting the Border States, he decided to attack slavery in the Confederacy.

THE FIRST INSTALLMENT

In the spring of 1862, Congress tackled slavery in the nation's capital city. There were roughly 3,000 slaves in Washington, DC. Massachusetts senator Henry Wilson introduced a bill to emancipate these slaves, compensating their owners with $300 per person.[3] Emotions exploded inside the halls of Congress and on the city streets. The mayor and members of the District of Columbia's city council begged legislators to reconsider the bill. If the capital city were free, these politicians feared fugitive slaves from Virginia and Maryland would flock there. The idea of a large, free black population made them nervous and fanned their racist paranoia. The city's leaders predicted Congress would be filled with blacks so that white women could not attend debates. They claimed an influx of free black men and women would make the capital city "a hell on earth for the

Senator Henry Wilson, who spent much of his time combatting slavery, proposed the Immediate Compensated Emancipation Act.

white man."[4] These white leaders could not envision living peacefully side-by-side with black people who were not enslaved.

Radical Republicans had their own agenda. They planned to emancipate the nation's slaves, step by step. The nation's capital was just the first step. Senator Charles Sumner claimed abolition in Washington, DC, "endanger[ed] slavery elsewhere."[5]

Lincoln did not like the bill because it freed slaves too quickly. He said, "Now families would at once be deprived of cooks, stable boys, etc, and they of their protectors without any provision for them."[6] The bill passed the legislature, and, despite reservations, Lincoln signed the Immediate Compensated Emancipation Act into law on April 16, 1862. The law immediately freed 3,104 people.[7]

STALLED ON THE PENINSULA

The Army of the Potomac, led by Union general George McClellan, spent the winter of 1862 camped around Washington. Lincoln repeatedly ordered McClellan to launch an offensive, but the general took his time. Finally, on March 17, McClellan ordered his army to move down the Potomac River to the Chesapeake Bay. He would advance up the Virginia Peninsula and attack the Confederate capital of Richmond. The launch down the Potomac River was spectacular: 120,000 soldiers, 300 cannons, 1,000 wagons, 15,000 mules and horses, and 400 ships.[8] A Union victory seemed certain.

But triumph turned into tragedy. Convinced he faced a massive Confederate army inside Yorktown, Virginia, McClellan hunkered down for a month-long siege. The small rebel force inside the city evacuated before McClellan attacked. The general resumed his march up the peninsula, but at a snail's pace. By the end of May, Union forces were within ten miles (16 km) of Richmond, but McClellan

FREEDOM IN THE CAPITAL

When slavery was abolished in Washington, DC, African Americans were jubilant. Frederick Douglass said, "I trust I am not dreaming."[9] Some freed blacks remained with their former masters and worked for wages, and others became cooks or valets in the army. A few weeks after this bill was passed, Congress changed the city's laws so African Americans could own their own businesses.

stalled again. Caught off-guard by his inaccurate estimates of the size of the Confederate forces defending Richmond, McClellan begged for reinforcements instead of attacking.

Meanwhile, the Confederate army had a bold, new commander—General Robert E. Lee. Lee noted McClellan's cautious nature. Although he had a much smaller army, Lee launched a surprise attack against Union forces on June 26 at the Battle of Mechanicsville. McClellan retreated, but Lee struck again and again. Over the course of the next week, the Union army backtracked down the peninsula. When they reached the shelter of the Union gunboats at Harrison's Landing, the Union had 16,000 casualties.[10] The Confederate casualty rate was higher, but Lee had saved Richmond, and the war raged on.

A CHANGE IN TACTICS

Lincoln despaired at McClellan's defeat but did not give up. He called for 300,000 more troops and declared, "I expect to maintain this contest until successful,

At the Battle of Mechanicsville, also known as the Battle of Beaver Dam Creek, Lee's Confederate army defeated McClellan's Union troops.

or till I die, or am conquered, or my term expires, or Congress or the country forsakes me."[12] However, Lincoln knew he needed to change his strategy. He later told artist Francis Carpenter, "I felt that we had . . . about played our last card, and must change our tactics, or lose the game."[13]

Republicans in Congress were already changing tactics. The Second Confiscation Act and its companion law—the Militia Act—were designed to give the Union army more power. The Confiscation Act made it legal for military commanders to seize the property of all Confederates and the property of those who gave support to rebels even if they were not directly involved in

SAILING TO FREEDOM

Fugitive slave Robert Smalls carried out one of the most spectacular acts of bravery in 1862. He was the slave pilot of the Confederate ship *The Planter*, and he was skilled in navigating dangerous or congested harbors and rivers. Smalls brought his family and other slaves aboard the vessel, disguised himself as captain, and steered the ship out of Charleston Harbor and into Union-held waters. The federal government made Smalls an officer in the US Navy, and after the war, Smalls served five terms in the US Congress.

fighting. This meant more slaves could be considered war contraband. The Militia Act authorized the president to use African Americans as laborers, soldiers, and sailors, and declared that any slave who performed such services would then be free.

Lincoln signed these bills on July 17, 1862, but he also sent a message to Congress, reminding lawmakers Congress had no authority to regulate slavery within a state. Frustrated at how reluctantly Lincoln moved on emancipation even when Congress handed him the legal authority, Republicans compared Lincoln to an old woman.

These critics were not aware Lincoln had been moving quickly in their direction. The lack of progress on the battlefield, the failure of the Border States to emancipate their slaves, and the incessant pressure from Radical Republicans to do more to end slavery led Lincoln to decide on a new war strategy. He met with his cabinet and read them a proclamation he had been drafting for weeks. Lincoln had resolved that on January 1, 1863, all slaves in the rebelling states

Lincoln met with his cabinet to read and discuss his drafted proclamation on July 22, 1862.

would "thenceforward, and forever, be free."[14] The president had concluded that to win the war, he must free the slaves.

Secretary of State William Seward issued a word of caution. If Lincoln made such an announcement on the heels of McClellan's disastrous campaign in Virginia, it would appear "as the last measure of an exhausted government, a cry for help."[15] Seward suggested Lincoln wait for a Union victory before issuing the proclamation. Lincoln agreed. The wait would be a long one.

The Union army was forced to retreat on August 30, 1862, at the Second Battle

WAITING TO ISSUE

Lincoln was desperate for a decisive military victory so he could issue the Emancipation Proclamation. After the Second Confiscation Act, many Americans expected Lincoln to issue some kind of emancipation declaration. But in August, the Union army suffered another defeat at the Second Battle of Bull Run. Lincoln remained silent. Horace Greeley, editor of the *New York Tribune*, printed "Prayer of Twenty Millions." In it, Greeley stated Lincoln was careless on the issue of freedom. Lincoln shot back with his own letter, which was published in papers throughout the country:

> *My paramount object in this struggle is to save the Union, and is not either to save or destroy slavery. If I could save the Union without freeing any slave I would do it, and if I could save it by*

freeing all the slaves I would do it; and if I could save it by freeing some and leaving others alone I would also do that. What I do about slavery, and the colored race, I do because I believe it helps to save the Union.[1]

The president was preparing the public for the announcement he would make just as soon as the war turned in the Union's favor.

JUSTIFICATION IN BLOOD

The military victory the president had been waiting for came on September 17, 1862. General Lee invaded Maryland, and the Union and Confederate armies tangled along the banks of Antietam Creek. The fighting began at 6:00 a.m. when Union batteries fired on Confederates who lay hidden in the woods on the far side of a cornfield.

The Battle of Antietam surged back and forth through the cornfield 15 times that day. A sunken lane ran down the middle of the Confederate front. From high ground, Union soldiers fired down into the rebel ranks. Bodies lay two to three deep, a sight that christened that road as "bloody lane."[2] At the end of the day, General Lee withdrew his army back into the South. The slaughter on both sides was horrific—more than 20,000 casualties for one day of war.[3] But the Union had stopped Lee's invasion of the North. Lincoln could claim a victory.

September 17, 1862, marked the bloodiest day in US history as the Battle of Antietam claimed thousands of Union and Confederate lives.

The president announced the preliminary Emancipation Proclamation on September 22. Hundreds of copies were sent to newspapers across the nation, and thousands more were distributed to the army for officers to read in the field.

CELEBRATION

Some abolitionists praised Lincoln for announcing the proclamation. Proponents held parades, bonfires, and rallies. But not all abolitionists were pleased. There were four million slaves in the United States in 1862. This proclamation only applied to 3.1 million of them.[4] Slaves in the Border States remained in bondage.

Democrats were also upset. The *New York Herald*, a Democratic newspaper, said emancipation would lead to racial insurrection and blacks would murder white men, women, and children. Ohio congressman Clement Vallandigham characterized Lincoln as a racial fanatic who was not uniting the Union but reinventing it according to his own vision.

Reaction from the troops in the field was as mixed as that of the nation. Some soldiers were eager to fight to free the slaves. Other soldiers supported the proclamation when they realized it might shorten the war.

SOLDIERS SUPPORT

Soldier John P. Jones from Illinois wrote to his wife, "The Year of Jubilee has come to the poor slave."[6] Private Levi Hines wrote that Lincoln was finally making war on slavery, and Hines was ready to sacrifice his life "for the purpose of ending that Hellish curse of our country."[7]

CONDEMNATION

Some soldiers condemned the proclamation. A Maryland private was sick of the war and even sicker of the fact that, instead of fighting for the freedom of the nation, he was fighting "for the freedom of the negroes."[5] Some of their commanders felt the same way. General Fitz-John Porter called the proclamation an act of cowardice. General McClellan told his troops that if they did not like the actions of their government, they must vote to change them.

Americans did turn out at the polls in the fall of 1862, and they dealt the Republican Party a harsh blow. Democrats gained control of state legislatures in Pennsylvania, Illinois, Indiana, Ohio, and New York, and gained seats in Wisconsin. New Jersey and New York elected Democratic governors. Race-baiting politicians contributed to the Republican loss by fostering hysteria among whites that free blacks would flood their towns and cities. Iowa and Indiana passed laws barring black people from migrating to their states.

General George McClellan considered resigning, convinced the proclamation would lead to massive slave revolts.

When the Confederates heard of the election results, they rejoiced, convinced the decrease in Republican power would lead to peace negotiations. But many of these slave owners had already lost their human property. Douglass declared the proclamation was already destroying slavery: "The negroes have heard of it, and are flocking in thousands to the lines of our army."[8] Owners moved their slaves deep into Southern territory so they could not flee to Union lines. But even then, the attitude of some slaves changed. One Alabama plantation mistress complained her slaves refused to do any chores because they claimed they were free.

RISKY RUN

Former slave Louis Hughes recorded the tragic fate of two slaves who were caught as they attempted to escape to Union lines. The other slaves at the plantation were lined up, and their owner described the gruesome details of the capture and execution of the two fugitives. Then the slaves were marched to the spot where the bodies of the runaways dangled from a tree limb. Blue flies swarmed around the corpses, and the stench of rotten flesh sickened Hughes. His owner wanted to discourage any other slaves from daring to reach for freedom.

CAUSE FOR CONCERN

Political and military pressure squeezed President Lincoln in a painful vice. As 1862 drew to an end, some people feared, and others hoped, Lincoln might modify, delay, or abandon the Emancipation Proclamation. Lincoln's own words led to this uncertainty. In his annual message to Congress on December 1, 1862, Lincoln introduced three constitutional amendments. The first amendment proposed that all states free their slaves by January 1, 1900, and be compensated with savings bonds. The second amendment declared all slaves who had already been freed by the war would remain free forever, and, if their owners were loyal to the Union, they would be compensated. The final amendment authorized Congress to appropriate the money needed to colonize any free blacks who volunteered to move to another country. Lincoln seemed to be trying to please all Northern whites, but he succeeded only in confusing them. People wondered what the proposed amendments meant for the Emancipation Proclamation.

Twelve days later, the Union army received a devastating blow. On December 15, General Ambrose Burnside tried to capture Confederate high ground near Fredericksburg, Virginia. General Lee's troops were shielded by the Heights, a 400-foot- (122 m) tall wall. Again and again, federal forces charged. The rebels repelled them. When the fighting stopped that evening, not a single Union soldier had breached the wall. The Union lost 12,000 men.[9]

Northern morale shattered. Desertion rates soared. People predicted Midwestern states would secede just to escape the war. In the last week of 1862, Democratic newspapers predicted Lincoln would abandon his promise to sign the Emancipation Proclamation on January 1, 1863.

Lincoln signed the final, official Emancipation Proclamation on January 1, 1863.

JUBILEE

On New Year's Day, 1863, Lincoln woke early, proofread the final draft of the Emancipation Proclamation, and sent it to the printing office. A copy was back on Lincoln's desk by 10:45 a.m. However, the printers had made an error. Lincoln sent the document back for correction. The signing would have to wait.

At 11:00 a.m., ushers opened the White House for a New Year's Day tradition. Citizens came by the hundreds to greet the president and his family, and Lincoln spent hours shaking hands. Finally, at 2:00 p.m., he slipped upstairs to his office. Some of his staff watched as he sat down at the large table. A document lay on the center of the table. Lincoln picked up a steel pen, its wooden handle gnawed during many hours of contemplation. He dipped the pen in the inkwell but then paused, his hand trembling. Lincoln set the pen down again and laughed. He was not nervous. Nor was he reconsidering. He had shaken so many hands that morning that his own was almost paralyzed.

The president rested his hand for a moment before taking the pen up again. "I never in my life," he told those gathered, "felt more certain that I was doing right than I do in signing this paper. . . . If my name ever goes into history it will be for this act, and my whole soul is in it. If my hand trembles when I sign the proclamation, all who examine the document hereafter will say 'He hesitated.'" Lincoln's days of hesitation were over. He signed his name across the bottom of the proclamation and laughed. "That will do," he said.[1]

A REVISED PROCLAMATION

The official Emancipation Proclamation made no mention of colonization. Perhaps Lincoln came to understand how degrading such a strategy was to black people who wanted to choose their own futures and how impractical such a strategy was. In January 1862, Frederick Douglass wrote an editorial, answering the question of what to do with the emancipated slaves: "Do nothing with them; mind your business, and let them mind theirs. . . . They have been undone by your doings, and all they now ask . . . is to just let them alone."[2] Lincoln never raised colonization as an option again.

Many opponents of emancipation feared former slaves would be angry and seek revenge. To appease these whites, the final version of the proclamation stated the Union army would not prevent slaves from making their own "suitable" efforts to gain freedom. Lincoln also appealed to slaves to avoid all "disorder, tumult, and violence" unless in self-defense.[3]

The most significant change between the preliminary proclamation and the final version was the clause permitting African Americans to join the armed services. While blacks had worked for the army and navy since the beginning of the war, they had served as contrabands or laborers who dug embankments, hauled supplies, cooked food, or heaved coal on ships. Now African Americans would be able to hold rifles.

The official Emancipation Proclamation issued on January 1, 1863, differed slightly from the draft Lincoln had announced the previous fall.

One change was small in size but huge in significance. In the preliminary proclamation, Lincoln had declared slaves in the rebelling regions "thenceforward, and forever free." However, he was not convinced he had the constitutional authority to declare slaves permanently free. Only a constitutional amendment—or at least a law passed by Congress—could absolutely abolish slavery. To make the Emancipation Proclamation as legal as possible, Lincoln changed the wording of the final version to read that slaves "henceforward shall be free."[4] The permanency of emancipation was not yet guaranteed.

IMPLEMENTATION

As president and commander in chief, Lincoln had the authority to take action for needs of war but could not change domestic policy without congressional action. Because the Emancipation Proclamation was a military measure, Lincoln could only free the slaves in regions the Confederacy controlled. Swaths of territory were exempt, including

CONFEDERATE REACTION

The Confederate government swiftly condemned the Emancipation Proclamation. President Jefferson Davis called the document "the most execrable measure recorded in the history of guilty man."[5] He said it would lead to either "the extermination of the slaves, [or] the exile of the whole white population of the Confederacy."[6] After the proclamation was issued, both sides knew peace talks were impossible. Events on the battlefield would determine the victor. By 1864, the rebel army was low on troops. Confederate President Davis proposed offering slaves their freedom if they fought for the South. The Confederate Congress authorized an emancipation bill, but only approximately 50 slaves signed on.[7]

Tennessee and parts of Louisiana, western Virginia, and the Border States, leaving approximately, 800,000 slaves in bondage. Three million slaves in the Confederacy were theoretically freed on January 1, 1863.[8]

The pace of actual emancipation depended on military victories, but slaves prepared for freedom. Some slaves played dumb so as to dupe their owners. Then slaves ran when they got the chance. Many owners did not give their slaves such a chance. Some states established housing camps for slaves far from Union lines. Slaves who could not run were freed when Union soldiers showed up with a copy of the Emancipation Proclamation in hand. In some places, this did not happen until the summer of 1865.

The proclamation impacted the Confederacy's ability to provide for its army and civilians. Slaves continued engaging in work slowdowns or refused to obey orders. These labor stoppages, coupled with drought and the huge amount of food the Confederate army consumed, meant prices for civilians skyrocketed.

In some areas of the Union-held South, life did not change much for slaves after the Emancipation Proclamation. Male slaves were recruited to join the military, but the elderly, women, and children continued to work on plantations run by the government or Northern land speculators. While the proclamation directed freed slaves should work for wages, some speculators refused to pay them.

Former slaves were victimized in the Border States. Large numbers of recently freed blacks intermingled with slaves in these states. Unscrupulous whites would seize any black person and declare him or her a fugitive from a Border State owner. The dealer would hold the person, supposedly until the owner claimed him or her. If no owner made a claim, the dealer would sell the black person on the auction block. This practice was notorious in Kentucky. In this way, some blacks who had just escaped slavery through the Emancipation Proclamation were re-enslaved.

TO ARMS, TO ARMS

Lincoln realized the potential African-American soldiers could have to change the trajectory of the war. In the fall of 1863, he wrote, "The bare sight of fifty thousand armed and drilled black soldiers on the banks of the Mississippi would end the rebellion at once."[9] Units of black soldiers had been formed under the guidelines of the Militia Act of 1862, but their numbers were small. By early 1863, the government was prepared to utilize the potential of black soldiers.

African Americans played a vital role in the ultimate Union victory. By the end of the war, 179,000 blacks served in the military, including 19,000 in the navy. Black troops composed 10 percent of the Union army. Sixty percent of these soldiers came from Confederate states and 25 percent from Border States.[10] By law, all black regiments were led by white officers, and black troops were paid only $10 a month compared to a white soldier's $13. Black soldiers performed valiantly. One-third of African-American soldiers died in the war from battle wounds or disease. Fifteen black soldiers and eight black sailors were awarded the Congressional Medal of Honor.[11]

Lincoln knew his decision to use black soldiers was correct. He wrote a letter to be read to a rally in Springfield, Illinois, in August 1863. In his letter, he stated, "Peace does not appear as distant as it did. . . . There will be some black men who can remember that, with silent tongue, and clenched teeth, and steady eye, and well-poised bayonet, they have helped mankind on to this great consummation."[12] The great consummation Lincoln referred to was the abolition of slavery. African-American soldiers helped the Union achieve victory on the battlefield. These victories ultimately ended the war and the institution of slavery.

EQUAL PAY FOR EQUAL WORK

In September 1863, Corporal James Henry Gooding wrote to President Lincoln asking why black troops were paid less than white soldiers. Gooding said if Lincoln questioned the quality of colored troops, he could dig up the mounds around Fort Wagner to find evidence of their bravery. Many black soldiers had died in a valiant effort to capture the Confederate stronghold at that South Carolina fort. In June 1864, Congress passed a law that ensured equal pay for all Union soldiers.

PHOTOS AS ABOLITIONIST TOOLS

Abolitionists used photographs to tell the story of slavery to a northern audience. In 1863, *Harper's Weekly* ran a story with three images of a slave called Gordon. The first photo showed Gordon as he appeared when he sought refuge behind Union lines in Louisiana. His ragged clothes were filthy from days spent fleeing from his owner and a pack of bloodhounds. The second photo stuns the viewer. Gordon sits sideways, one hand on his hip. His back is furrowed with a maze of scars from a whipping he received on Christmas Day. The third image shows Gordon in the uniform of the Union army, a musket in his hands.

The article touts Gordon's "unusual intelligence and energy."[13] Abolitionists sold this image and devoted the proceeds to raising money to educate freed blacks. *The Scourged Back*, as Gordon's photo was called, shamed and horrified northern viewers. The *New York Independent* said the photograph "should be multiplied by 100,000 and scattered over the states" because it told "the story [of slavery's brutality] to the eye."[14]

A TYPICAL NEGRO.

We publish herewith three portraits, from photographs by M'Pherson and Oliver, of the negro GORDON, who escaped from his master in Mississippi, and came into our lines at Baton Rouge in March last. One of these portraits represents the man as he entered our lines, with clothes torn and covered with mud and dirt from his long race through the swamps and bayous, chased as he had been for days and nights by his master with several neighbors and a pack of blood-hounds; another shows him as he underwent the surgical examination previous to being mustered into the service—his back furrowed and scarred with the traces of a whipping administered on Christmas-day last; and the third represents him in United States uniform, bearing the musket and prepared for duty.

This negro displayed unusual intelligence and energy. In order to foil the scent of the blood-hounds who were chasing him he took from his plantation onions, which he carried in his pockets. After crossing each creek or swamp he rubbed his body freely with these onions, and thus, no doubt, frequently threw the dogs off the scent.

At one time in Louisiana he served our troops as guide, and on one expedition was unfortunately taken prisoner by the rebels, who, infuriated beyond measure, tied him up and beat him, leaving him for dead. He came to life, however, and once more made his escape to our lines.

By way of illustrating the degree of brutality which slavery has developed among the whites in the section of country from which this negro came, we append the following extract from a letter in the New York *Times*, recounting what was told by

the refugees from Mrs. GILLESPIE'S estate on the Black River:

The treatment of the slaves, they say, has been growing worse and worse for the last six or seven years.

Flogging with a leather strap on the naked body is common; also, paddling the body with a hand-saw until the skin is a mass of blisters, and then breaking the blisters with the teeth of the saw. They have "very often" seen slaves stretched out upon the ground with hands and feet held down by fellow-slaves, or lashed to stakes driven into the ground for "*burning*." Handfuls of dry corn-husks are then lighted, and the burning embers are whipped off with a stick so as to fall in showers of live sparks upon the naked back. This is continued until the victim is covered with blisters. If in his writhings of torture the slave gets his hands free to brush off the fire, the burning brand is applied to them.

Another method of punishment, which is inflicted for the higher order of crimes, such as running away, or other refractory conduct, is to dig a hole in the ground large enough for the slave to squat or lie down in. The victim is then stripped naked and placed in the hole, and a covering or grating of green sticks is laid over the opening. Upon this a quick fire is built, and the live embers sifted through upon the naked flesh of the slave, until his body is blistered and swollen almost to bursting. With just enough of life to enable him to crawl, the slave is then allowed to recover from his wounds if he can, or to end his sufferings by death.

"Charley Sloo" and "Overton," two hands, were both murdered by these cruel tortures. "Sloo" was whipped to death, dying under the infliction, or soon after punishment. "Overton" was laid naked upon his face and burned as above described, so that the cords of his legs and the

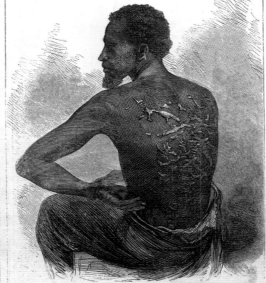

GORDON AS HE ENTERED OUR LINES.

GORDON UNDER MEDICAL INSPECTION.

GORDON IN HIS UNIFORM AS A U. S. SOLDIER.

THE EMANCIPATION PROCLAMATION'S EFFECTS

Independence Day, 1863, was like none other. On July 1, rebel forces had skirmished with outnumbered Union troops at the small town of Gettysburg, Pennsylvania. Overnight, reinforcements from both sides converged onto the scene, and the battle over the next two days seemed to encompass the universe. Union casualties were 23,000 compared to the Confederates' 28,000.[1] But the Union could replace these troops while the rebels could not. On July 4, the Confederate army limped back into Virginia, and the Union army buried their dead.

Meanwhile, in the west, General Ulysses S. Grant also dealt the Confederates a heavy blow on Independence Day. Vicksburg sat on the bluffs overlooking the Mississippi River. For weeks, Grant had laid siege to this Confederate stronghold. Residents survived on rations of rats, mule meat, and sugarcane sprouts. On the morning of July 4, the Confederate army raised white flags above the city, announcing its surrender.

These twin triumphs in the summer of 1863 demonstrated the war had turned in the North's favor. Although the bloodshed was far from over, the Union army slowly advanced toward victory, and the Emancipation Proclamation transformed the nation.

ENFORCER OF EMANCIPATION

In his third annual message to Congress in December 1863, Lincoln was so confident the rebellion was crumbling that he proposed terms by which the Confederate states could rejoin the Union. One requirement was that rebels were to take an oath to obey all proclamations and laws abolishing slavery.

Lincoln spoke too soon. The war was long from over. Bloody confrontations occurred at Chickamauga and Chattanooga in 1863. The slaughter continued in 1864 at places whose names evoked a scarred landscape: Wilderness, Cold Harbor, and the Crater. However, even as casualty rates rose, the end of war was in sight. In 1864, Lincoln appointed General Ulysses S. Grant to command all

The Union victory at Vicksburg severed the Confederacy in two.

Union armies, and Grant selected William Tecumseh Sherman to help command. In September, Sherman's troops captured Atlanta, Georgia, and then he led an army of 60,000 on a 285-mile (460 km) march to Savannah. Sherman brought the war to the doorsteps of Southern civilians.

Georgia's fertile red soil fed the Confederate army, and Georgia's slaves tilled that earth. Sherman's army targeted both sources of Confederate strength. This

During what became known as Sherman's March to the Sea, Union troops destroyed Confederate land and property in their path.

action was justified under both the Emancipation Proclamation and the Lieber Code, a set of war rules Lincoln had adopted in 1863 that allowed the Union army to destroy civilian property to win the war. The troops were ordered to forage ahead. Georgian crops, livestock, and warehouses were fair game, and the army consumed the countryside like a voracious beast. All slaves in the Union path were emancipated, and thousands attached themselves to Sherman's army. Sherman put some freed slaves to work, while others tagged along at the fringes of his army, afraid to get too close but reluctant to remain among the rebels.

In November 1864, Northerners went to the polls to elect a president. Lincoln had been convinced he would lose. However, news of Sherman's progress through Georgia buoyed the public. Lincoln was reelected by a wide margin. And on December 21, 1864, Sherman presented the city of Savannah to President Lincoln as a Christmas present. The Confederacy was taking its last breaths.

TRAINING GROUND FOR FREEDOM

With emancipation, African Americans had to transition from the life of a slave to one of a free person. Military experience helped some make the psychological shift this required. Black soldiers helped teach the concepts of liberty and justice to slaves. A white man was a sergeant in the First Regiment, US Colored Troops. In 1864, he was stationed near Jamestown, Virginia. His unit captured a slave owner who had recently whipped some of his female slaves. A soldier in the unit was a former slave of the same owner. This soldier ordered the owner tied to a tree. First he whipped

EMANCIPATION IN THE BORDER STATES

Military service was the most direct route to freedom for slaves in the Border States. On October 1, 1863, General Orders No. 329 authorized the military to recruit all able-bodied males. For slaves who were not men of fighting age, the path to emancipation was slower. Republicans gained control of the state legislatures in Maryland and Missouri and drafted new state constitutions that abolished slavery. Maryland's went into effect on November 1, 1864, and Missouri's in January 1865. Both Delaware and Kentucky resisted all efforts toward emancipation until required to comply with them by the ratification of the Thirteenth Amendment in December 1865.

the owner, and then he handed the whip over to the slave women. The tables of justice had been turned.

Following the Emancipation Proclamation, blacks began fighting for broader freedoms. The State Central Committee of Colored Men of Michigan petitioned the Michigan legislature to abolish laws that made reference to skin color. In Illinois, blacks worked to overturn a law banning African Americans from moving to the state. In California, they petitioned to change a law preventing blacks from testifying against whites in court, and in Philadelphia, blacks challenged the city's segregated streetcars, which were eventually integrated in 1867.

In March 1863, the American Freedmen's Inquiry Commission investigated the conditions of emancipated blacks to see what they needed to become self-supporting people. The investigation concluded the former slaves were loyal to their country; they had faith in their government and wanted to work for wages. But what they needed most was proof of their freedom. That proof came with the Thirteenth Amendment.

THE END OF SLAVERY FOR ALL TIME

The only way to permanently abolish slavery throughout the nation was to amend the Constitution. In the winter of 1864, Congress began debating such an amendment. Democrats argued ending slavery would lead to interracial sexual relationships and black equality. Republicans countered that the amendment would do nothing more than give blacks freedom from enslavement. The amendment needed two-thirds of the votes in both houses to go to the states for ratification. It achieved that in the Senate but fell short in the House. When Lincoln was reelected in November 1864, he used all his presidential power to convince congressmen.

Lincoln's efforts paid off. The House passed the Thirteenth Amendment by a margin of two votes. The Constitution requires that three-fourths of the states also approve any changes to the document. The amendment was sent to the states for ratification, and on December 6, 1865, slavery was abolished throughout the United States.

The House of Representatives celebrated after the passing of the Thirteenth Amendment.

LEGACIES

On April 4, 1865, President Lincoln sauntered through the recently captured city of Richmond. Black workers dropped to their knees at the sight of him, crying "Father Abraham's come." Lincoln reprimanded them. "Don't kneel to me," he said. "You must kneel to God only, and thank him for the liberty you will hereafter enjoy."[2]

That liberty was soon a reality for all slaves. On April 9, General Robert E. Lee surrendered his Army of Northern Virginia to General Ulysses S. Grant at Appomattox, Virginia. Although there were other skirmishes, the Civil War essentially ended with this act. But less than a week later, Abraham Lincoln was dead, shot by an assassin's bullet.

The Emancipation Proclamation was a temporary war measure, but it led to a permanent freedom that did not end with the president's death. The groundwork for the proclamation had been laid by scores of people across numerous decades. Lincoln, the self-taught lawyer, found a way to free the slaves in accordance with

JUNETEENTH

On June 19, 1865, two months after the war had essentially ended with General Lee's surrender at Appomattox, Union General Gordon Granger arrived in Galveston, Texas. Granger informed the slaves in the state that they were free, something they did not yet know. The slaves sang, danced, and celebrated. Although June 19 is not a legal holiday, the majority of states and Washington, DC, recognize Juneteenth as a day of independence.

the Constitution he had sworn to uphold. He insisted the war was to save the Union. But he came to realize he could not save the Union without also freeing the slaves. Emancipation began as a means to an end, but so transformed the war that the abolition of slavery became an end in and of itself. The Emancipation Proclamation went farther than any other law had gone before. It recognized African Americans as people instead of property, and the order applied to all slaves in the rebelling lands, not just slaves that belonged to rebel masters.

EMANCIPATION MEMORIAL

In 1876, the Emancipation Memorial, financed in part by former slaves, was dedicated to Abraham Lincoln. Thomas Ball, a white man, designed the statue. Lincoln stands, a rolled-up document in his hand. A black man wearing a forlorn expression kneels at Lincoln's feet. Some African Americans found the sculpture insulting, as though they had no hand in obtaining their own freedom. In 1998, the African American Civil War Memorial was erected a few miles away. Three black Union soldiers and one black Union sailor stand erect, their jaws set with determination. The soldiers carry muskets. These two monuments—separated by a century—reflect the nation's evolving views of emancipation.

Over time, the Emancipation Proclamation tarnished. After a decade of progress following the Civil War, former Confederates and the planting elite regained power in the South, and Black Codes limited the freedom of African Americans in the South for another century. These codes prevented blacks from voting, serving on juries, testifying against whites, or owning guns. Additionally, blacks had to be employed by whites, and in some states, blacks were barred from owning land. The Emancipation Proclamation was a promise to the nation's black

EMANCIPATION

The Emancipation Memorial, *left*, and the African American Civil War Memorial, *right*, show different depictions of the African-American role in emancipation.

people. When white supremacy reasserted itself in the South, African Americans realized this promise would not be fulfilled easily or quickly.

However, the promise did not disappear. Freed from the shackles of slavery, African Americans began to more broadly define what it meant to be free. Blacks battled for basic rights—the right to own land, to go to school, to ride public transportation, to get a job, to vote—year after year, decade after decade. As one man from California said after the Emancipation Proclamation was issued, "Old things are passing away, and eventually old prejudices must follow. The revolution has begun, and time alone must decide where it is to end."[3] The Emancipation Proclamation launched that revolution. It remains in progress.

THE FIGHT TO END SEGREGATION CONTINUES

On August 28, 1963, civil rights activist Reverend Dr. Martin Luther King Jr. stood on the steps of the Lincoln Memorial and delivered his famous "I Have a Dream" speech. In 1963, public facilities across the South were segregated. Many states denied blacks the right to vote, and racial violence was rampant. King called on President John F. Kennedy to issue a proclamation that immediately outlawed all forms of discrimination and segregation. Kennedy was assassinated first. His successor, Lyndon Johnson, supported two key civil rights laws. The Civil Rights Act of 1964 outlawed segregation in public accommodations and the Voting Rights Act of 1965 banned all racial barriers to voting. Both laws helped fulfill the promise of the first Emancipation Proclamation.

TIMELINE

August 1619

The first African-American captives arrive in colonial North America.

September 17, 1787

The Constitution is signed.

September 1829

The publication of David Walker's *Appeal* marks the beginning of the abolitionist movement.

November 6, 1860

Abraham Lincoln is elected president.

September 1861

President Lincoln revokes General John Frémont's order emancipating slaves in Missouri.

April 16, 1862

The Immediate Compensated Emancipation Act abolishes slavery in the District of Columbia.

July 17, 1862

Congress passes the Second Confiscation Act, permitting African Americans to serve in the military.

September 17, 1862

The Battle of Antietam ends in a Union victory.

December 20, 1860

South Carolina secedes from the United States.

April 12, 1861

The Civil War begins with the Battle of Fort Sumter.

May 1861

Union General Benjamin Butler grants fugitive slaves refuge at Fort Monroe, declaring them contraband of war.

August 6, 1861

Congress passes the First Confiscation Act.

December 6, 1865

The Thirteenth Amendment is ratified, abolishing slavery throughout the United States.

September 22, 1862

The preliminary proclamation is issued.

January 1, 1863

The final Emancipation Proclamation is issued.

April 9, 1865

General Robert E. Lee surrenders to General Ulysses S. Grant, signaling the end of the Civil War.

ESSENTIAL FACTS

KEY PLAYERS

- President Abraham Lincoln governed the Union.

- President Jefferson Davis governed the Confederacy.

- General Robert E. Lee was the primary commander of the Confederate army.

- General Ulysses S. Grant eventually led the Union army to victory.

POLITICAL TURNING POINTS

- The First Confiscation Act authorized the Union to confiscate slaves whom the Confederates used for military purposes.

- The Second Confiscation Act authorized the Union to use African Americans in the military and to seize property belonging to anyone who supported the Confederacy, even if the person was not directly engaged in the war.

- The preliminary Emancipation Proclamation gave notice that President Lincoln planned to free the slaves of all rebelling states in the New Year.

- The final Emancipation Proclamation declared slaves in rebelling states free and authorized the recruitment of African Americans into the military.

- The passage of the Thirteenth Amendment abolished slavery throughout the nation.

MILITARY TURNING POINTS

- A Union defeat at the First Battle of Bull Run pushed Congress to pass the First Confiscation Act.

- A Union victory at the Battle of Antietam permitted President Lincoln to release the preliminary Emancipation Proclamation.

- Sherman's March to the Sea resulted in the liberation of thousands of slaves and broke the morale of the Confederates.

IMPACT

The Emancipation Proclamation transformed the Civil War from a conflict aimed at preserving the Union to a war for the liberation of slaves.

QUOTE

"I never in my life . . . felt more certain that I was doing right than I do in signing this paper. . . . If my name ever goes into history it will be for this act, and my whole soul is in it."

—*Abraham Lincoln on signing the Emancipation Proclamation, January 1, 1863*

GLOSSARY

ABOLITIONIST
A person who wants to end slavery.

AMENDMENT
A formal addition or change to a document.

CABINET
The president's key advisers.

COLONIZE
To take over an area of land by sending people to settle that land.

COMPENSATION
Money given to cover lost or damaged property.

CONTRABAND
A slave who, during the Civil War, escaped or was brought within Union lines.

DEHUMANIZE
To treat someone as though he or she is not a human being.

EMANCIPATION
The act of freeing an individual or group from slavery.

EXEMPT
Not required to do something that others are required to do.

FUGITIVE
A person who runs away to avoid recapture.

INDENTURED SERVANT
A person contracted to work for a certain period of time, usually without pay.

INSURRECTION
A hostile rebellion.

MILITIA
A military force made up of nonprofessional fighters.

PETITION
To make a formal request.

SECEDE
To formally withdraw from a political union.

ADDITIONAL RESOURCES

SELECTED BIBLIOGRAPHY

Brewster, Todd. *Lincoln's Gamble: The Tumultuous Six Months That Gave America the Emancipation Proclamation and Changed the Course of the Civil War.* New York: Scribner, 2014. Print.

Klingaman, William K. *Abraham Lincoln and the Road to Emancipation: 1861–1865.* New York: Viking, 2001. Print.

Masur, Louis. *Lincoln's Hundred Days: The Emancipation Proclamation and the War for the Union.* Cambridge, MA: Harvard UP, 2012. Print.

Willis, Deborah, and Krauthamer, Barbara. *Envisioning Emancipation: Black Americans and the End of Slavery.* Philadelphia, PA: Temple UP, 2013. Print.

FURTHER READINGS

Krensky, Kevin. *The Emancipation Proclamation.* Cavendish Square, 2011. Print.

McGruder, Kevin, and Thomas Velma Maia. *Emancipation Proclamation: Forever Free.* Chicago, IL: Urban Ministries, 2013. Print.

WEBSITES

To learn more about Essential Library of the Civil War, visit **booklinks.abdopublishing.com**. These links are routinely monitored and updated to provide the most current information available.

PLACES TO VISIT

Antietam National Battlefield
5831 Dunker Church Road
Sharpsburg, MD 21782
301-432-5124
http://www.nps.gov/anti/index.htm
Tour the ground that was the site of the bloodiest day in US history. The Union victory at Antietam led President Lincoln to issue the preliminary Emancipation Proclamation.

Frederick Douglass National Historic Site
1411 W Street SE
Washington, DC, 20020
202-426-5961
http://www.nps.gov/frdo/index.htm
Visit Cedar Hill, the home where former slave and abolitionist Frederick Douglass lived from 1877 to 1895.

SOURCE NOTES

CHAPTER 1. WATCH NIGHT

1. "Emancipation Proclamation." *History*. History, n.d. Web. 4 Nov. 2015.

2. "Fredericksburg." *Civil War Trust*. Civil War Trust, n.d. Web. 4 Nov. 2015.

3. Kevin McGruder and Thomas Velma Maia. *Emancipation Proclamation: Forever Free*. Chicago, IL: Urban Ministries, 2013. Print. 74.

4. David Brion Davis. *The Problem of Slavery: In the Age of Emancipation*. New York: Knopf, 2014. Print. 15.

5. "Emancipation Proclamation." *National Archives*. National Archives and Record Administration, n.d. Web. 4 Nov. 2015.

6. Louis Masur. *Lincoln's Hundred Days: The Emancipation Proclamation and the War for the Union*. Cambridge, MA: Harvard UP, 2012. Print. 208.

7. Ibid. 217–218.

8. Allen C. Guelzo. "The Emancipation Proclamation: Bill of Lading or Ticket to Freedom?" *History Now*. The Gilda Lehrman Institute of American History, n.d. Web. 14 Nov. 2015.

CHAPTER 2. SLAVERY AS AN INSTITUTION

1. "African Americans at Jamestown." *National Park Service*. National Park Service, n.d. Web. 1 Nov. 2015.

2. "Virginia Recognizes Slavery." *Africans in America*. PBS, n.d. Web. 1 Nov. 2015.

3. "Colonial Laws." *Africans in America*. PBS, n.d. Web. 1 Nov. 2015.

4. "Petition 1/13/1777." *Africans in America*. PBS, n.d. Web. 1 Nov. 2015.

5. "The Declaration of Independence." *Digital History*. Digital History, n.d. Web. 14 Nov. 2015.

6. "Rough Draft of the Declaration of Independence." *Africans in America*. PBS, n.d. Web. 1 Nov. 2015.

7. "The Revolutionary War." *Africans in America*. PBS, n.d. Web. 1 Nov. 2015.

8. Ibid.

9. "Growth and Entrenchment of Slavery." *Africans in America*. PBS, n.d. Web. 1 Nov. 2015.

10. "Ten Facts about Washington and Slavery." *Mount Vernon.org*. Mount Vernon Ladies' Association, n.d. Web. 4 Dec. 2015.

11. Eric Foner. *Forever Free: The Story of Emancipation and Reconstruction*. New York: Knopf, 2005. Print. 16–17.

12. "'A Slave is Tortured.'" *Africans in America*. PBS, n.d. Web. 1 Nov. 2015.

13. "The Compromise of 1850 and the Fugitive Slave Act." *Africans in America*. PBS, n.d. Web. 1 Nov. 2015.

CHAPTER 3. EARLY EMANCIPATION EFFORTS

1. "The Underground Railroad." *Africans in America*. PBS, n.d. Web. 3 Nov. 2015.

6. Louis Masur. *Lincoln's Hundred Days: The Emancipation Proclamation and the War for the Union*. Cambridge, MA: Harvard UP, 2012. Print. 219.

3. Bryan Walls. "Freedom Marker: Courage and Creativity." *PBS*. PBS, n.d. 3 Nov. 2015.

4. "Nat Turner's Rebellion." *Africans in America*. PBS, n.d. Web. 3 Nov. 2015.

5. "The *Liberator*: 'To the Public.'" *Africans in America*. PBS, n.d. Web. 5 Nov. 2015.

6. "Angelina Grimké Weld's Speech at Pennsylvania Hall." *Africans in America*. PBS, n.d. Web. 5 Nov. 2015.

7. "Emigration and Colonization: The Debate Among African Americans, 1780's–1860's." *National Humanities Center Resource Toolbox*. National Humanities Center, n.d. Web. 4 Nov. 2015.

8. "American Colonization Society (1816–1964)." *BlackPast*. BlackPast.org, n.d. Web. 6 Nov. 2015.

CHAPTER 4. SLAVERY SPLITS THE NATION

1. "Diary of Mary Chesnut: Crisis at Fort Sumter." *Civil War Trust*. Civil War Trust, n.d. Web. 6 Nov. 2015.

2. Ibid.

3. "Bleeding Kansas." *Africans in America*. PBS, n.d. Web. 7 Nov. 2015.

4. "Cooper Union Address." *Abraham Lincoln Online*. Abraham Lincoln Online, n.d. Web. 7 Nov. 2015.

5. Louis P. Masur. "Liberty Is a Slow Fruit: Lincoln the Deliberate Emancipator." *American Scholar* 81.4 (2012): 44–53. *Academic Search Premier*. Web. 12 Oct. 2015.

CHAPTER 5. TO SAVE THE UNION

1. William K. Klingaman. *Abraham Lincoln and the Road to Emancipation: 1861–1865*. New York: Viking, 2001. Print. 47.

2. Louis P. Masur. "Thenceforward and Forever Free, Mostly." *Washington Monthly* 45.1/2 (2013): 11–14. *Academic Search Premier*. Web. 12 Oct. 2015.

3. Eric Foner. *Forever Free: The Story of Emancipation and Reconstruction*. New York: Knopf, 2005. Print. 44–45.

4. Adam Goodheart. "How Slavery Really Ended in America." *New York Times Magazine*. New York Times, 1 Apr. 2011. Web. 6 Nov. 2015.

5. Ibid.

6. "The First Battle of Manassas." *Civil War Series*. National Park Service, n.d. Web. 8 Nov. 2015.

7. Kate Masur. "Slavery and Freedom at Bull Run." *New York Times*. New York Times, 27 July 2011. Web. 6 Nov. 2015.

8. Harold Holzer, Edna Greene Medford, and Frank J. Williams. *The Emancipation Proclamation: Three Views*. Baton Rouge: Louisiana State UP, 2006. Print. 12.

9. Steve Moyer. "Remarkable Radical: Thaddeus Stevens." *Humanities*. National Endowment for Humanities, Nov./Dec. 2012. Web. 5 Dec. 2015.

10. "Congressional Debate." *Civil War*. Lehrman Institute, n.d. Web. 5 Dec. 2015.

11. William K. Klingaman. *Abraham Lincoln and the Road to Emancipation: 1861–1865*. New York: Viking, 2001. Print. 85.

CHAPTER 6. A MILITARY MEASURE

1. Louis Masur. *Lincoln's Hundred Days: The Emancipation Proclamation and the War for the Union*. Cambridge, MA: Harvard UP, 2012. Print. 45.

SOURCE NOTES CONTINUED

2. William K. Klingaman. *Abraham Lincoln and the Road to Emancipation: 1861–1865*. New York: Viking, 2001. Print. 107.

3. Louis Masur. *Lincoln's Hundred Days: The Emancipation Proclamation and the War for the Union*. Cambridge, MA: Harvard UP, 2012. Print. 47.

4. William K. Klingaman. *Abraham Lincoln and the Road to Emancipation: 1861–1865*. New York: Viking, 2001. Print. 118.

5. Ibid.

6. Ibid. 119.

7. Hari Jones. "The Road to Emancipation." *Civil War Trust*. Civil War Trust, n.d. Web. 6 Nov. 2015.

8. William K. Klingaman. *Abraham Lincoln and the Road to Emancipation: 1861–1865*. New York: Viking, 2001. Print. 120.

9. Ibid. 111.

10. Ibid. 138.

11. Harold Holzer, Edna Greene Medford, and Frank J. Williams. *The Emancipation Proclamation: Three Views*. Baton Rouge: Louisiana State UP, 2006. Print. 19.

12. William K. Klingaman. *Abraham Lincoln and the Road to Emancipation: 1861–1865*. New York: Viking, 2001. Print. 138.

13. Louis P. Masur. "Liberty Is a Slow Fruit: Lincoln the Deliberate Emancipator." *American Scholar* 81.4 (2012): 44–53. *Academic Search Premier*. Web. 12 Oct. 2015.

14. Todd Brewster. *Lincoln's Gamble: The Tumultuous Six Months that Gave America the Emancipation Proclamation and Changed the Course of the Civil War*. New York: Scribner, 2014. Print. 73–74.

15. H. W. Brands. "Hesitant Emancipator." *American History* 44.2 (2009): 54–59. *Academic Search Premier*. Web. 12 Oct. 2015.

CHAPTER 7. WAITING TO ISSUE

1. Harold Holzer. "A Promise Fulfilled." *Civil War Times* 48.6 (2009): 28–35. *Academic Search Premier*. Web. 12 Oct. 2015.

2. Geoffrey C. Ward. *The Civil War: An Illustrated History*. New York: Knopf, 1990. Print. 159.

3. Ibid. 223.

4. Louis P. Masur. "Thenceforward and Forever Free, Mostly." *Washington Monthly* 45.1/2(2013): 11–14. *Academic Search Premier*. Web. 12 Oct. 2015.

5. William K. Klingaman. *Abraham Lincoln and the Road to Emancipation: 1861–1865*. New York: Viking, 2001. Print. 200.

6. Louis Masur. *Lincoln's Hundred Days: The Emancipation Proclamation and the War for the Union*. Cambridge, MA: Harvard UP, 2012. Print. 131.

7. Ibid. 132.

8. Ibid. 136.

9. William K. Klingaman. *Abraham Lincoln and the Road to Emancipation: 1861–1865*. New York: Viking, 2001. Print. 218.

CHAPTER 8. JUBILEE

1. Harold Holzer. "A Promise Fulfilled." *Civil War Times* 48.6 (2009): 28–35. *Academic Search Premier*. Web. 12 Oct. 2015.

2. Louis P. Masur. "Liberty Is a Slow Fruit: Lincoln the Deliberate Emancipator." *American Scholar* 81.4 (2012): 44–53. *Academic Search Premier*. Web. 12 Oct. 2015.

3. Todd Brewster. *Lincoln's Gamble: The Tumultuous Six Months that Gave America the Emancipation Proclamation and Changed the Course of the Civil War.* New York: Scribner, 2014. Print. 232.

4. Ibid. 235.

5. Bruce Catton. "Inescapable Challenge Lincoln Left Us." *Lincoln Monographs.* University of Michigan, n.d. Web. 6 Nov. 2015.

6. William K. Klingaman. *Abraham Lincoln and the Road to Emancipation: 1861–1865.* New York: Viking, 2001. Print. 236.

7. Louis Masur. *Lincoln's Hundred Days: The Emancipation Proclamation and the War for the Union.* Cambridge, MA: Harvard UP, 2012. Print. 260.

8. Harold Holzer, Edna Greene Medford, and Frank J. Williams. *The Emancipation Proclamation: Three Views.* Baton Rouge: Louisiana State UP, 2006. Print. 20.

9. Louis Masur. *Lincoln's Hundred Days: The Emancipation Proclamation and the War for the Union.* Cambridge, MA: Harvard UP, 2012. Print. 222.

10. Ibid.

11. Eric Foner. *Forever Free: The Story of Emancipation and Reconstruction.* New York: Knopf, 2005. Print. 52.

12. Louis Masur. *Lincoln's Hundred Days: The Emancipation Proclamation and the War for the Union.* Cambridge, MA: Harvard UP, 2012. Print. 246.

13. "Gordon as He Entered Our Lines." *Library of Congress.* Library of Congress, n.d. Web. 13 Nov. 2015.

14. Deborah Willis and Barbara Krauthamer. *Envisioning Emancipation: Black Americans and the End of Slavery.* Philadelphia, Temple UP, 2013. Print. 37.

CHAPTER 9. THE EMANCIPATION PROCLAMATION'S EFFECTS

1. "Gettysburg." *CWSAC Battle Summaries.* National Park Service, n.d. Web. 4 Nov. 2015.

2. William K. Klingaman. *Abraham Lincoln and the Road to Emancipation: 1861–1865.* New York: Viking, 2001. Print. 287.

3. Eric Foner. *Forever Free: The Story of Emancipation and Reconstruction.* New York: Knopf, 2005. Print. 58.

INDEX

ABOUT THE AUTHOR

Judy Dodge Cummings is a writer and former history teacher from Wisconsin. Some of her other books include *The American Revolution: Experience the Battle for Independence*, *Civil War*, and *Human Migration: Investigate the Global Journey of Humankind*.